I0060519

BUSINESS WAIT LOSS

A GUIDE TO HELP ENTREPRENEURS END THE CYCLE OF PROCRASTINATION AND TAKE ACTION

KARYN BUGGS

Eagle Eye Publishing

Business Wait Loss is a kick in the butt, all-in-one workbook and guide that will lead you out of procrastination and into action for the achievement of your goals and realization of your dreams.

Copyright © 2013 Karyn Buggs

ISBN: 978-0-615857-10-7

ALL RIGHTS RESERVED
No part of this book may be reproduced or transmitted in any form or by any means: graphic, electronic or mechanical, including photocopying, recording, taping or by any information storage and retrieval system, without permission in writing from the author, except for the inclusion of brief quotations in a review.

Eagle Eye Publishing
Bedford Hts., OH

Cover Design by Jermel Wilkerson, Sr. - www.jwilksr.com
Interior Design by Same Page Graphics & Marketing Solutions, LLC.

Photo Credits:
© 2013 Shilah Kidd
© Olga Vasilkova | Dreamstime Stock Photos (page 52)
© Galina Barskaya | Dreamstime Stock Photos (page 52)
© Harvey Burchett - www.harveyryanphotography.com (page 62)
© Nspimages | Dreamstime Stock Photos (page 102)

Dedication

This book is dedicated to my husband, Cordelle Buggs, who encouraged me to take my own advice, stop talking and take action!

CONTENTS

Acknowledgements

To my parents, Hugh & Peggy Kidd, who never allowed me to fit in with the "popular" crowd and constantly encouraged me to do better than the time before.

I offer much love to the creative genius on this project, my daughter, Shilah. Thank you for your support, encouragement, feedback and talent you shared in the creating of this book.

To my son, Cyre, thank you for just being you. You inspire me to keep going even when I feel like giving up!

I will always be grateful to Johnny B. Jones and Bobbie Jones for believing in me and supporting my endeavors. Thanks to my friends and family who hold me accountable, expect me to rise above the norm and always look forward to my next big endeavor.

A special note of thanks to the students, entrepreneurs and business professionals I've educated, coached, mentored or consulted. You inspire me to learn more, create more and be more.

The Challenge

The completion of this book is the result of a mother-daughter challenge.

At the end of the second quarter of my daughter's sophomore year, I gave her my usual advice about working hard and putting forth 100% to achieve her goals. But this time, I also added the need to push past your comfort zone and do things that are uncomfortable in order to be your best.

At the time, I had already been encouraged to write this book, but writing was definitely outside my comfort zone. My daughter & I also discussed a few things outside her comfort zone that would help achieve her best.

The challenge was on! We both agreed that in the next 45 days we would both do things outside our comfort zone. And so it was, the lesson taught, the challenge accepted, and action began. Business Wait Loss was born.

Introduction

This book is for the person with a desire to start a business or get past the plateau all entrepreneurs experience in the beginning stages. If you're looking for a bunch of success stories, this book isn't for you. Reading other people's stories might be inspiring but creating your own story is life changing! This book gets straight to the point so that you can take action and start creating.

Here's how it works. There are 5 sections that represent areas of high importance when starting your business. Refer back to these sections at any time. The pictures represent a thousand words you don't have to read.

The quotes and their interpretation summarize various business concepts. The mnemonics make the information easy to absorb and remember. The most important part is that you take action. So, after each concept you have an opportunity to document actionable items and a *plan of execution*. You will create your *daily achievement list* from your plan of execution.

Throughout the book there are bold and italicized words. You can find the meaning of these words in the glossary on page 124.

My core message to you is LOSE THE WAIT and TAKE ACTION! There is no greater thief of business potential than procrastination.

SECTION 1

Visionary Tools

The way that you think has an impact on everything you do. This section is packed with wisdom to help you improve your thinking and shift to a growth mindset.

Once you have developed it, you will find that staying on task and taking action towards positive business growth will be second nature.

"A journey begins
with a single step."

Unknown

Without taking a step forward, nothing is achieved because you are at a standstill. Even the longest and most difficult ventures have a starting point. Take the initiative and start moving today. Here's how:

S et a priority level for your goals.

T ie each priority to an emotional value.

E veryday do at least one thing toward achieving your goals.

P ush yourself to do at least one uncomfortable task daily.

"Most of us spend too much time on what is urgent and not enough time on what is important."

– Stephen R. Covey

💡 Idea Sparkers:

Write at least 3 reasons why you want to start this business or why you've already started one.

Think about how you will feel when you accomplish this goal.

When this happens, how will your life change and how will you change the lives of others?

👣 Actionable Item & Plan of Execution:

Priority levels help you decide what to do first and what can wait until later or be delegated to others.

Define a 3 level priority system.
- ☐ Decide on the labels A, B, C or 1, 2, 3.
- ☐ Schedule time to write descriptions for each priority level which will also help you visualize what you plan to achieve.
- ☐ Determine the order of priority, ascending or descending.

Actionable Items

_____

_____

_____

_____

_____

Choose one actionable item and write your plan of execution?

_____

_____

_____

_____

_____

_____

_____

_____

_____

"Information is the gatekeeper to power."

Excerpt from Gung Ho

With the right information and access to the right resources, you have the power to achieve anything.

I nform other like-minded individuals of your vision, goals, and dreams.

N etwork outside of your circle.

F ind people in your industry that you can ask for help.

O penly sharing information with others is the key to unleashing the power.

💡 Idea Sparkers:

Make a list of networking groups in your area and people you respect in the industry.

Invite positive energy into your space by letting go of the fear of someone stealing your idea. One of the most effective ways to do this is by being aware of scarcity thinking. If you become conscious of the abundance of potential that is available to everyone, you will soon find that you no longer fear your competition.

Manifesting your idea starts by seeing it in your head, saying it out loud, and writing it down.

👣 Actionable Item & Plan of Execution:

Attend one networking event
- ☐ Choose at least 2 best days and times.
- ☐ Research network groups to find a good fit for you.
- ☐ Select a network event that fits your needs and schedule
- ☐ Register or RSVP your attendance.
- ☐ Add the event and times to your calendar.
- ☐ Draft a networking plan which should include who you want to meet, what you want from them, what you will say and how you will follow up.

Actionable Items

_____

_____

_____

_____

_____

Choose one actionable item and write your *plan* of execution?

_____

_____

_____

_____

_____

_____

_____

_____

_____

"Mistakes are valuable. You can't learn anything from being perfect."

Adam Osborne

When you make a mistake in business, you learn what works and what doesn't. Don't repeat what doesn't work but keep trying until you find what does work. That's learning from your mistakes.

M istakes give you permission to be human.

I dentify ways you can make adjustments and improvements.

S tart documenting your mistakes and your solutions; they'll be profitable later.

T rue expertise is gained from making mistakes and learning how to resolve them.

A void thinking that mistakes are bad.

K eep reframing your thinking about mistakes.

E xpect to make mistakes often because nobody is perfect.

"I have not failed. I've just found 10,000 ways that won't work."
-Thomas A. Edison

💡 Idea Sparkers:

Write down 5 positive thoughts that you can reflect on when you feel like you've failed and be conscious of how good the thoughts make you feel. (i.e. Mistakes are a necessary part of learning. I now have a better idea of how to handle this situation.)

Write a story about your biggest mistake, what you learned, and what adjustments you made to ensure you didn't repeat it.

👣 Actionable Item & Plan of Execution:

Reflect on my mistakes
- ☐ Choose a day and time to reflect.
- ☐ Purchase a journal and special pen.
- ☐ Answer the question above and document what I have learned from this mistake?
- ☐ Be honest about why I feel bad about making mistakes.

Actionable Items

_____

_____

_____

_____

_____

Choose one actionable item and write your plan of execution?

_____

_____

_____

_____

_____

_____

_____

_____

"Failure is a prerequisite
to learning."

Eric Ries

Do not view failure as a negative. All people fail at something in their lives and most commonly, failures happen in business. Although painful, failing allows you to see areas needing improvement, reveals lessons about how to plan for next time, and gives you the skills to change to meet the needs of your customer.

F ocus on the discovery of reasons for the failure, not on the fact that you failed.

A lign yourself with people who will support and encourage you when you fail.

I dentify and prepare for potential problems before they arise.

L earning to fail early gives you the ability to rapidly try and test out new ideas and discard the ones that don't work.

"Failure is simply the opportunity to begin again, this time more intelligently."

– Henry Ford

💡 Idea Sparkers:

Who has encouraged you when you've failed?

How can you prepare for potential problems before they occur?

What are the potential problems you may encounter during this journey?

👣 Actionable Item & Plan of Execution:

Establish a support system
- ☐ Make a list of people who encourage and cheer me on.
- ☐ Share my vision with this list of people.
- ☐ Let my cheerleaders know that I will reach out to them throughout this journey.
- ☐ Make a separate list of "talk me off a cliff" supporters.

Actionable Items

_____

_____

_____

_____

_____

Choose one actionable item and write your plan of execution?

_____

_____

_____

_____

_____

_____

_____

_____

SECTION 2

Barriers to Entry

You may experience resistance, obstacles, and self-doubt. This section provides motivation, tips and tools for you to properly prepare and overcome these barriers.

"Soon is not as good as now."

Seth Godin

There is no perfect time to start. Your idea may not be fully developed, but do something every day to move forward. Waiting to pursue your dreams will eventually turn into never pursuing your dreams.

Never is there a "perfect time".

Others need your gifts and talents.

Write down the goals and dreams you've been putting off.

💡 Idea Sparkers:

What is the one thing you know you've been putting off?

What are the reasons? (Example: "Now isn't a good time.")

What's the worst that could happen if you started now?

👣 Actionable Item & Plan of Execution:

Figure out what's stopping me
- ☐ Answer the question: What am I afraid of?
- ☐ Make a list of the things or situations I believe are holding me back.
- ☐ Make a list of the people who will benefit from my dream becoming a reality.
- ☐ Answer this question: Why is now not good time?

Actionable Items

_____

_____

_____

_____

_____

Choose one actionable item and write your plan of execution?

_____

_____

_____

_____

_____

_____

_____

_____

_____

"Stop making excuses
and make moves."

Karyn Buggs

There will always be lots of reasons why you shouldn't move forward with your goals or dreams. Decide to move forward even if you don't have all the information. You'll find the information as you move along your journey.

M otivation: find what motivates you to keep going and do that often.

O verwhelming feelings are diminished when you have an *accountability partner*.

V isible: keep your dreams and goals in front of you.

E very great player needs a great *coach*, *mentor*, or *sponsor*.

💡 Idea Sparkers:

Who do I know that has traveled this journey?

What motivates me? (Hint: Money should not be a motivator)

What makes me feel relaxed and helps me think with a clear head?

👣 Actionable Items & Plan of Execution:

Find a mentor, coach and sponsor
- ☐ Look in the glossary to know the difference in these roles.
- ☐ Make a list of potential candidates.
- ☐ Make a list of what I expect from each person.
- ☐ Contact each person to set up a meeting.
- ☐ Develop an agenda for the meeting.

Actionable Items

_____

_____

_____

_____

_____

Choose one actionable item and write your plan of execution?

_____

_____

_____

_____

_____

_____

_____

_____

"Change your mindset,
change your world."

Karyn Buggs

Your mind dictates your actions, and your feelings and behavior follow your thoughts. So program yourself to believe you can achieve your goals. What happens when you decide to think positively? You'll begin to see things differently; you'll react to things differently; your conversation is will be different; and you'll get different responses from those around you.

C reate affirmations out of your own self doubt.

H andwrite your affirmations.

A void words or phrases like "try", "I can't", "it's hard", "I'll never", "hopefully".

N eed the support of other like minds? Join a network group.

G ive yourself permission to be imperfect.

E xperience the change.

💡 Idea Sparkers:

Focus on what you're really good at doing.

Replace your self-doubt with positive affirmations.

👣 Actionable Item & Plan of Execution:

Develop a plan for positive thinking
- ☐ Handwrite positive affirmations.
- ☐ Post the affirmations around the work area and in the bathroom.
- ☐ Carry a copy of my affirmations with me or store them in my phone.
- ☐ Schedule time to think about the self-doubt triggers.
- ☐ Develop a plan to handle these triggers.

Actionable Items

_____

_____

_____

_____

_____

Choose one actionable item and write your plan of execution?

_____

_____

_____

_____

_____

_____

_____

_____

_____

"It's better to hang out with people different from you."

Karyn Buggs

Observe and learn from people who think differently, act differently, network differently, speak differently, or live in different places. You may actually find a new and better way to do something!

Do something outside of your comfort zone.

Intentionally spend time with people who are not like you.

Fitting in is not the goal; learning is the goal.

Full potential is achieved by setting higher standards.

Evaluate your existing circle.

Relationship building is vital to moving forward.

Engage in learning by doing.

Network on purpose.

Think BIGGER and enlist the help of others that have different skills.

💡 Idea Sparkers:

What makes you most uncomfortable when networking?

How can you make your goal or dream bigger?

With whom should you build relationships in order to get this thing going?

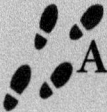

👣 Actionable Items & Plan of Execution:

Talk to 5 people about my business
- ☐ Determine what I expect from the people to whom I talk.
- ☐ Set aside time to craft a message.
- ☐ Make a list of 5 people to whom I could talk.
- ☐ Schedule time, if needed, to talk to them.

Actionable Items

_____

_____

_____

_____

_____

Choose one actionable item and write your plan of execution?

_____

_____

_____

_____

_____

_____

_____

_____

_____

"Develop your business like you drive a car."

Karyn Buggs

Driving a car requires constant course corrections, while launching a rocket requires careful and detailed planning. While some planning is necessary in business, your efforts should be put into what and when adjustments are needed. This means you are listening to your customers.

C onstantly make minor adjustments based on customer feedback.

A ct as if you're experimenting and exploring solutions to your customers' needs and problems.

R *epeatable processes* make it easy to duplicate your actions, measure results and make corrections.

💡 Idea Sparkers:

Are you spending too much time planning and not enough time testing your idea with customers?

What assumptions have you made about the results from using your product or service?

What value do you deliver to customers?

What do you believe is the benefit of using your product or service?

👣 Actionable Items & Plan of Execution:

Develop a feedback loop for feasibility of my idea
- ☐ Look up the definition of feedback loop.
- ☐ Develop a list of questions for the survey.
- ☐ Research free survey tools.
- ☐ Create an account for survey tools.
- ☐ Determine how many survey responses I will use to analyze information.
- ☐ Schedule time to review results.
- ☐ Input questions into survey tool.
- ☐ Send out or post a survey on social media.

Actionable Items

_____

_____

_____

_____

_____

Choose one actionable item and write your plan of execution?

_____

_____

_____

_____

_____

_____

_____

_____

_____

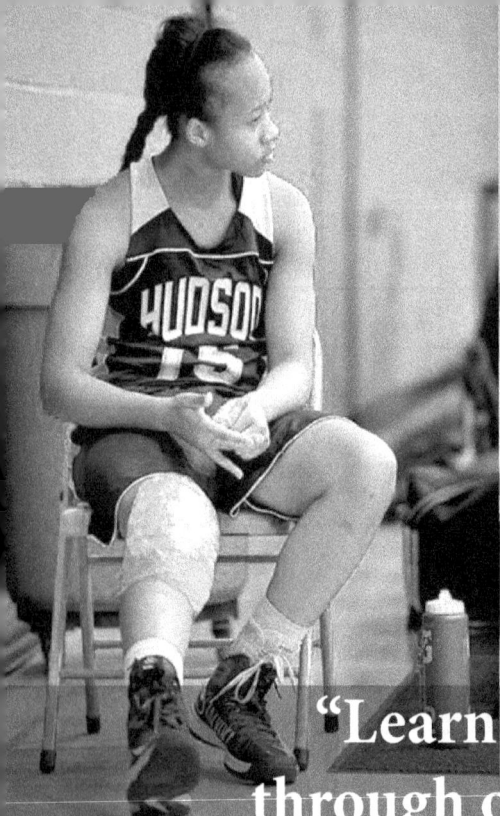

"Learn to play through obstacles."

Karyn Buggs

Business is one of the toughest paths you can take in life! There will be challenges, but there are just as many rewards. Your ability to move forward and accomplish goals even when it hurts will be the difference in the success you experience.

P ersistence is critical to progress.

L earn to have fun; it will make the challenges easier to bear.

A lways celebrate accomplishments.

Y ou aren't alone; others have been there and done that. Seek them out for inspiration.

💡 Idea Sparkers:

What or who inspires you?

How do you celebrate accomplishments?

How much do you want to make this idea or dream real?

What have you done in the past to move beyond an obstacle?

👣 Actionable Item & Plan of Execution:

Do at least one thing daily for my business
- ☐ Develop a master list of items from my plans of execution.
- ☐ Schedule one thing from this list every day.

Actionable Items

_____

_____

_____

_____

_____

Choose one actionable item and write your plan of execution?

_____

_____

_____

_____

_____

_____

_____

_____

_____

SECTION 3

Take Action

This section is all about making procrastination productive. It addresses common reasons for procrastinating and presents strategies to help you get moving.

"Don't ask a golfer
how to swing a bat."

Jeff Hoffman

Asking the right people for advice is important if you want to get the best information. Get suggestions from people who have been where you are and who have gone where you're going.

S tay true to your authentic self. Be careful of those trying to change your voice or vision.

W here you want to go has been traveled already. Create your road map.

I mmerse yourself in learning about the industry.

N egative thinkers have no room in the house of progress.

G et involved with people who do what you want to do.

💡 Idea Sparkers:

How do you want your business to look and feel?

Knowing how you want to be known in your business will help you remain authentic and true to yourself.

Be sure you are asking the right questions.

👣 Actionable Items & Plan of Execution:

Find 3 people in my industry for inspiration
- ☐ Set aside time to research people in my industry or in my community.
- ☐ Make a list of questions I need answered.
- ☐ Choose at least one person I can reach out to for help.
- ☐ Develop a plan before meeting with them.

Actionable Items

_____

_____

_____

_____

_____

Choose one actionable item and write your plan of execution?

_____

_____

_____

_____

_____

_____

_____

_____

"Too many of us are not living our dreams because we are living our fears."

Les Brown

Fear, an emotion induced by a perceived threat, becomes a problem when you allow it to keep you from living out your dream(s). Don't allow fear to be the obstacle that stands in your way. If you know what causes your fear, you can plan to do something about it!

L ife will happen with or without you.

I dentify all the positive things that will result from living your dream.

V ictory is yours when you choose it.

E very fear is connected to something you believe is true. What if you believe the opposite?

💡 Idea Sparkers:

What positive words describe your personality?

Be honest about what you are afraid will happen if you live your dream?

Start identifying the triggers for your thoughts and fears.

👣 Actionable Item & Plan of Execution:

Start the day with a positive mindset
- ☐ Write out positive words and phrases.
- ☐ Post positive words or phrases in the bathroom, kitchen, workspace, and near the door I exit.
- ☐ Allot time to meditate and visualize myself living out my dream.

Actionable Items

_____

_____

_____

_____

_____

Choose one actionable item and write your plan of execution?

_____

_____

_____

_____

_____

_____

_____

_____

_____

"Nothing beats a failure
but a TRY!"

Dell Buggs

Trying is better than not trying at all!! Not trying at all gives you a 100% chance of failing. Don't give up before you try; give yourself the best chance to achieve your goals by trying!

Trust your instincts.

Reach beyond your circle of comfort for assurance.

YES! Just say YES to your goals and dreams.

💡 Idea Sparkers:

Thinking of people who support you may not push you past your limits. This is your circle of comfort. You need someone to hold you accountable to your commitment.

A feeling of uneasiness about change usually means you're on the right track.

Embrace the fact that your instinct has power.

👣 Actionable Item & Plan of Execution:

Define what makes me uncomfortable
- ☐ Make a list of things that make me feel uncomfortable.
- ☐ Identify any common themes.
- ☐ Acknowledge why these things make me feel uncomfortable.

Actionable Items

_____

_____

_____

_____

_____

Choose one actionable item and write your plan of execution?

_____

_____

_____

_____

_____

_____

_____

_____

"If you can dream it
you can do it...this started
with a dream and a mouse."

Walt Disney

Within you exists the very thing(s) to make your dreams a reality. Don't sit back and let your dreams pass by or be passed along to someone else. All grand ideas started with a dream or a vision!

D ecide you will do it.

R elationships: build and nurture them.

E ngage others who have the power or resources to help you make it happen.

A ction: take it consistently and with the right mindset.

M *onetize* your idea; without it, it's still a dream.

💡 Idea Sparkers:

Dwell on those things that fill your heart with joy and excitement when you think about doing them.

Think about how you feel when you're not doing these things.

👣 Actionable Items & Plan of Execution:

Determine what's holding me back
- ☐ Set aside quiet time to reflect.
- ☐ Make a list of the things I think are keeping me from acting on my dreams.
- ☐ Choose one thing from the list to tackle.
- ☐ Develop a plan on how to tackle this one thing.
- ☐ Commit to tackling the obstacle.

Actionable Items

_____

_____

_____

_____

Choose one actionable item and write your plan of execution?

_____

_____

_____

_____

_____

_____

_____

_____

"Your business model is greater than your business idea."

Unknown

Your business model shows how and why your business should work. Business models make a realistic evaluation of your business potential; identifying revenue sources, customer base and sources of financing. It's your business idea in action.

Map out a plan of how and why your business will work.

Ongoing testing and measuring will help keep you on track.

Develop a cost structure and income stream.

Explain what value you deliver to your customers.

Listen to the needs of your customers and respond by making improvements and adjustments.

💡 Idea Sparkers:

Consumers aren't eager to buy what others aren't buying.

You should be able to sustain business operations and make a profit in order to appeal to the market.

Which ideas will realistically make money?

Be sure to think about this before spending a lot of time fine tuning the idea.

👣 Actionable Items & Plan of Execution:

Develop a business model
- ☐ Write down all the ways I can make money with my idea.
- ☐ Choose one idea to start with.
- ☐ Start testing this model with customers via surveys, sales or crowdfunding. Crowdfunding is a way to raise small amounts of money from a large number of people. (i.e. $10 from 500 people to raise $5000 for a startup or civic project).

Actionable Items

_____

_____

_____

_____

_____

Choose one actionable item and write your plan of execution?

_____

_____

_____

_____

_____

_____

_____

_____

_____

SECTION 4

Pump Up The Volume

When you start feeling alone, frustrated, annoyed and overwhelmed, this section will inspire you to kick it up another notch.

"You are the average of the five people you spend the most time with."

Jim Rohn

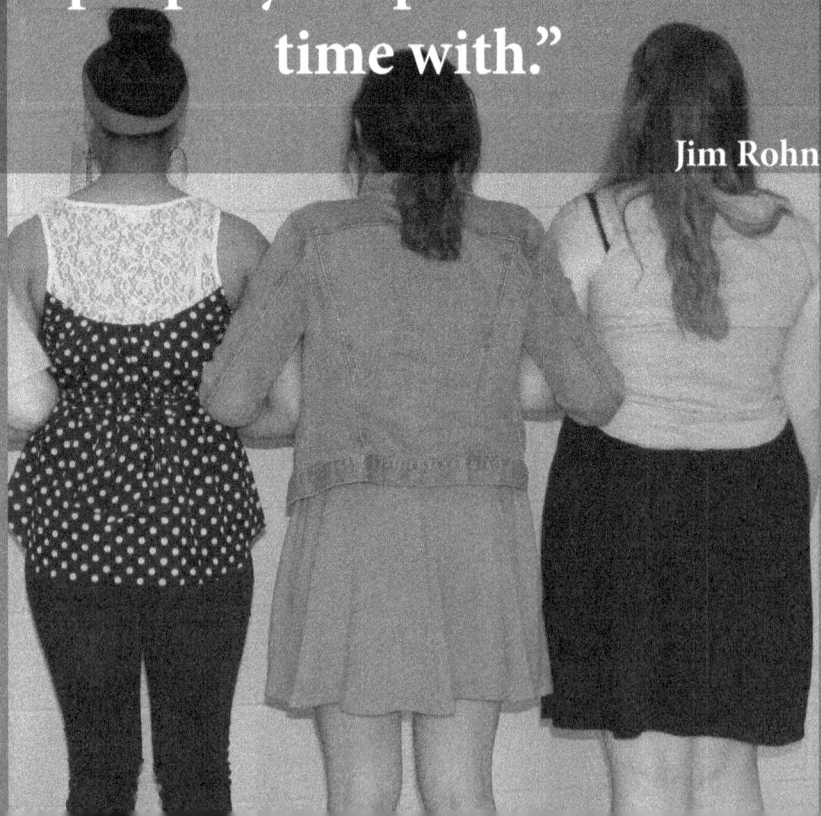

The people you surround yourself with have influence over your thoughts, actions, and behavior. Will they help you get to the next level?

F orget about trying to fit in; follow your heart and be authentic.

I dentify how the people who you spend time with can help you to the next level.

V alue your time and how much it is worth.

E valuate your relationships and ask if they are healthy or hurtful?

💡 Idea Sparkers:

How do you behave and act when you're among your circle of comfort?

What does being authentic and true to yourself mean to you?

What is the next level for you and who do you know that can help you get there?

👣 Actionable Item & Plan of Execution:

Identify the characteristics and personality of my fave five
- ☐ Set aside time to reflect.
- ☐ Write down the 5 people I spend the most time with.
- ☐ Attach an adjective and a verb to each person.
- ☐ Answer this question for each: How do I act and feel when I interact with this person?

Actionable Items

_____

_____

_____

_____

_____

Choose one actionable item and write your plan of execution?

_____

_____

_____

_____

_____

_____

_____

_____

"Don't fall in love with the solution; fall in love with the problem."

Unknown

Don't get attached to your *"**revolutionary**"* idea for solving a problem in the marketplace. The market may not respond favorably to your proposed solution, so be open to changing it. Focus on the problem you see in the marketplace and generate different solutions.

P ain points of your customers will reveal many different solutions.

R eevaluate your solution to ensure it aligns with your *target market*.

O pportunities for change; look for them.

B e prepared to change direction.

L ook for opportunities to collaborate with others in the same market.

E xercise creative problem solving.

M eet the needs of the customer, not your ego.

💡 Idea Sparkers:

What problem will you solve or what need will you fill?

Think about the many other solutions already on the market for this problem or need.

What other ways can you solve this problem or fill this need?

Can you solve this problem for another market?

👣 Actionable Items & Plan of Execution:

Identify pain points of my customer/client
- ☐ Give myself permission to be wrong with my current solution.
- ☐ Commit to finding the right solution for the marketplace.
- ☐ Develop a list of pain points/needs my customer may have.
- ☐ Ask at least 100 customers if they would purchase my solution to solve their problem.

Actionable Items

_____

_____

_____

_____

_____

Choose one actionable item and write your plan of execution?

_____

_____

_____

_____

_____

_____

_____

_____

_____

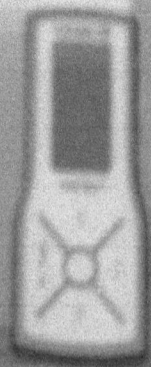

"There are no original ideas, just original actions."

Andre Abrams

There are over 7 billion people in the world. Most ideas are not new and may already be on the market, but you don't need new ideas to "make it". However, you do need to act on your idea to make progress and see accomplishments!

A lready there are ideas that can be improved upon.

C hoosing something already on the market can be a better option than trying to be the first.

T ap into what's already working and make it your own.

💡 Idea Sparkers:

Consider the various brands of water, chips, search engines, computers, etc we currently use and what makes each different.

Think about what determines your buying decisions?

Are there other variations of your idea in the market?

👣 Actionable Item & Plan of Execution:

Learn to take imperfect action
- ☐ Embrace the fact that my idea isn't original.
- ☐ Document at least 5 ways to make my initial idea different.
- ☐ Decide to take action on one of the 5 ideas.

Actionable Items

_____

_____

_____

_____

_____

Choose one actionable item and write your plan of execution?

_____

_____

_____

_____

_____

_____

_____

_____

"Excuses are arguments for your limitations."

Unknown

Excuses limit your ability to be persistent. When you make excuses you are telling yourself I can't or I won't achieve my goals or dreams. Push yourself beyond your limits and experience limitless possibilities.

P lan to do a little more than the time before.

U nderstand your weaknesses and work to manage them.

S top being complacent, BE MORE.

H ow have others reached where you want to go? Do your research and then make it your own.

💡 Idea Sparkers:

Consider how far along you'd be if you started when you first thought of the idea.

What are some smaller steps you can take to lead up to the big idea?

What do you consider to be your limitations?

👣 Actionable Item & Plan of Execution:

Intentionally push myself beyond my limits
- ☐ Complete these statements: I can't _____, I don't know how to ____, and I don't have the time to _____.
- ☐ Consider why I have set these limits.
- ☐ Address the reasons I've set these limits.
- ☐ Reword my statements to: I will _____, I am good at _____, I will make time to _____.
- ☐ Make a promise to do something from my reworded list daily.

Actionable Items

_____

_____

_____

_____

_____

Choose one actionable item and write your plan of execution?

_____

_____

_____

_____

_____

_____

_____

_____

SECTION 5

Breaking the Rules

Stepping outside your own comfort zone is necessary if you want to see remarkable changes. This section gives you insight into doing something different and how to throw away your own box.

"Success is not a group exercise; it's individual."

Karyn Buggs

Don't measure your success based on the thoughts, opinions or success of others. Your success should only be measured by the accomplishment of the goals you set for yourself.

S top trying to get approval from others.

U se your energy to believe you can and will.

C ontrol your own destiny.

C hange as you grow and learn.

E xamine what you want and value; money doesn't always mean success.

S tructure your goals and dreams around what you love.

S pend your time working on things important to you.

💡 Idea Sparkers:

Whatever you've assumed about the success of others, believe the same is possible for you.

Meditate daily about what true success looks like for you.

👣 Actionable Item & Plan of Execution:

Document my accomplishments
- ☐ Set aside time to reflect on the last 30 days.
- ☐ Document everything I have accomplished no matter how big or small.
- ☐ Have a celebration and share your success with others.

Actionable Items

_____

_____

_____

_____

_____

Choose one actionable item and write your plan of execution?

_____

_____

_____

_____

_____

_____

_____

_____

_____

"A good plan today is better than a perfect plan tomorrow."

George S. Patton

Recognize that your skills, your resources, your cash, your time, and your dream or idea is sufficient enough to get started now! There isn't any such thing as perfection in this world. If you always wait until you have a perfect plan, your time will eventually run out.

T rust yourself.

O pen your mind.

D edicate a portion of your day to taking action on your goals.

A llow yourself to be perfectly imperfect.

Y ou do need a plan, just not a perfect one.

💡 Idea Sparkers:

What can you do to get started now?

Think of the concept of how you make a sandwich, follow a recipe, or tie your shoes.

Reflect on your skills and the resources you can access.

👣 Actionable Item & Plan of Execution:

Take inventory of my skills and resources
- ☐ Set aside time to reflect.
- ☐ Make a list of my skills, how much cash I can realistically allot to my idea, any outside resources I can access, and how much time I am committed to devote on a monthly basis.
- ☐ Prepare a SWOT analysis using the list created to analyze and evaluate my strengths, weaknesses, opportunities and threats.
- ☐ Use the analysis to help me determine my competitive advantage, address any weaknesses or create new services and products.

Actionable Items

_____

_____

_____

_____

_____

Choose one actionable item and write your plan of execution?

_____

_____

_____

_____

_____

_____

_____

_____

_____

"A business without sales is a hobby."

Karyn Buggs

Making sales is what makes a business a business. It's nice to talk about your business but it's imperative to make sales in the business to survive. If you're not spending time selling your product or service, then you may just want to admit it's something you like to do for fun!

S elling doesn't mean being pushy.

E valuate the sales you need in order to break even.

L earn how to sell and market or partner with someone who knows how.

L everage the power of social media.

💡 Idea Sparkers:

How much have I sold? Why or why not?

How do I feel about making money from this idea?

Am I building relationships?

How comfortable am I with selling?

👣 Actionable Items & Plan of Execution:

Develop a system for building relationships
- ☐ Identify my ideal client.
- ☐ Make a list of people I know that can help me share my message.
- ☐ Contact each individual on my list to set up a coffee date to get acquainted (this is not a sales date).
- ☐ Enter the date in my calendar.
- ☐ Develop a list of questions I want to ask (get curious about them versus focusing on what you want from them).
- ☐ Confirm the date the day before.
- ☐ Follow up with something of value (i.e. an article, a book, a connection).

Actionable Items

_____

_____

_____

_____

Choose one actionable item and write your plan of execution?

_____

_____

_____

_____

_____

_____

_____

_____

"Traction speaks louder than words."

Karyn Buggs

You can talk about how awesome and *revolutionary* your product or service is, but how does your *target* customer respond? Customer response and income are good indicators of the momentum of growth. Consequently, investors are attracted to sales, not the big idea.

T rack and record your sales.

R eaching your target is essential; how will you market to them?

A lways start with *low hanging fruit*.

C onfidence to sell is a MUST.

T alk isn't cheap; especially if that's all you're doing. Get out and sell and stop talking about it.

I dentify your target market and what makes them buy.

O utside your comfort zone is where the "magic" happens.

N eed to be clear and confident in your business before you start to sell.

💡 Idea Sparkers:

Consider people or businesses in your community that would benefit from your solution.

In what areas are you lacking confidence?

Imagine you have a bullhorn to communicate your solution to a large crowd. What crowd do you want to listen?

👣 Actionable Items & Plan of Execution:

Identify your *low hanging fruit*
- ☐ Make a list of people and business that would benefit from your solution.
- ☐ For each person or business on the list, write down how your product or service will help solve their problem or fill a need.
- ☐ Develop a plan to reach them to begin building the relationship.
- ☐ Research any missing information such as contact person, phone numbers or email addresses.

Actionable Items

_____

_____

_____

_____

_____

Choose one actionable item and write your plan of execution?

_____

_____

_____

_____

_____

_____

_____

_____

_____

"A year from now you will wish you had started today."

Karen Lamb

There is no perfect time to pursue your dreams. Start doing the things your heart has been calling you to do. When you witness someone living out a similar dream, you'll have regrets. When you make the decision to finally live out your dream, you'll regret not doing it sooner. Live without regrets and get started now!

S tart with small ideas and work your way to the bigger things.

T ruth is someone needs your special gifts and talents.

A llow yourself to be honest about what's holding you back and ask for help.

R ules, there are none; just make it happen.

T ake action daily.

💡 Idea Sparkers:

If you had assurance everything would work out as you plan, what would you be doing?

Who needs the special gifts and talents only you possess?

Consider the impact your work will have on those closest to you and the legacy you'll leave behind.

👣 Actionable Item & Plan of Execution:

Determine my starting point
- ☐ Set aside time to do some deep thinking.
- ☐ Document everything that comes to mind during this deep thinking session (fears, obstacles, joys, dreams, unfulfilled dreams, etc). You may begin to notice a common theme.
- ☐ Choose an idea or goal to begin executing.
- ☐ Develop a vision statement for the idea or goal.
- ☐ Consider ways to scale the vision to smaller steps.
- ☐ Choose the first step or a starting point.
- ☐ Intentionally set aside time to do one thing every day.

Actionable Items

_____

_____

_____

_____

_____

Choose one actionable item and write your plan of execution?

_____

_____

_____

_____

_____

_____

_____

_____

_____

"If you can't explain it simply, you don't understand it well enough."

Albert Einstein

Being able to explain something in simple terms forces you to think precisely and consistently and to articulate a strategy. When you explain things in simple terms, your idea is clear and fuzzy thinking gets exposed and discarded.

S aying too much can cause confusion about your idea.

I mpressions are made in the first few seconds, make it memorable.

M essage map your idea for simplicity and clarity.

P ractice pitching your idea to friends, strangers, supportive and hostile listeners.

L isten to other pitches for improvement or what not to do.

E nd your message with a call to action. What do you want the listener to do?

💡 Idea Sparkers:

How long does it take you to explain your idea?

Can you draw a picture of your concept?

Does your current explanation cause a sideways look of confusion when explained?

Your message needs to be explained when you're not around.

👣 Actionable Item & Plan of Execution:

Attend a business pitch competition or presentation
- ☐ Research and make a list of accelerators, incubators, business colleges, entrepreneur organizations and libraries in my area that support entrepreneurship.
- ☐ Check out their calendar or call to visit and inquire about pitch competitions, classes or workshops.

Actionable Items

_____

_____

_____

_____

_____

Choose one actionable item and write your plan of execution?

_____

_____

_____

_____

_____

_____

_____

_____

_____

SO NOW WHAT?

I am so proud that you have decided to lose the wait and take decisive action toward achieving your goals and dreams. Now, I want to celebrate with you.

Send an email to BWL@KarynBuggs.com and let me know what progress you've made and how Business Wait Loss has helped you in your business. Be sure to put 'Celebrate with Me' in the subject line.

Send as many celebration emails as you wish. By submitting your testimonial, you give www.KarynBuggs.com permission to use all or part of it on our website or promotional materials.

We are not meant to figure everything out for ourselves. The bible encourages us in Ecclesiastes 4:9-12 to put our collective heads together and help each other deal with whatever life presents; and not just during challenging times.

I look forward to hearing how Business Wait Loss has worked for you!

Heart to Heart,

Karyn

GLOSSARY

Accountability partner – a person to help you keep your commitments.

Actionable item – a documented event or task that needs to take place.

Coach – an individual that offers expert advice and guidance to help move your business forward, usually for a fee.

Daily achievement list – a list of tasks derived from your plan(s) of execution that you expect to complete.

Low hanging fruit – the most obvious opportunities or the easiest to reach target in which to market your product or service.

Mentor – an individual that has been where you're trying to go and helps you follow a similar path through support and guidance.

Monetize – make money from selling your product or service.

Plan – a documented method you will use to accomplish a goal/objective.

Plan of execution – a documented list of the detailed and specific steps to happen in order to complete an actionable item.

Target – a specific group of people that you choose to provide a service or product.

Target market – a specific group of people to whom you will advertise and promote your product or service.

Repeatable Process – set of action steps to allow for consistency of results and efficient use of resources.

Revolutionary – brings about a major change.

Sponsor - an individual that uses their power to open doors and advocate on someone's behalf.

ABOUT THE AUTHOR

Karyn Buggs is a thought leader, an agent of change, and an optimist. She believes in the ability to build a better world with other like-minded people.

Described as a results-oriented thinker with a rare style of teaching, Karyn educates business leaders on how to get their greatest work out into the world. With a bold goal to build a world in which the vast majority view problems as possibilities and opportunities, Karyn is leading a movement to help people reframe their mindset, launch their dreams and reignite their passion.

An accountant by training and education with a career in real estate, Karyn is the author of Business Wait Loss, a guide and workbook to help the should've, could've and would've thinkers to lose their wait and take action now. She has a passion for seeing others accomplish their goals and achieve the dreams that once seemed unattainable. Karyn is fascinated by the human brain, how it works, and why we do the things we do. She has discovered the patterns of why people procrastinate, and she thrives on developing simple, manageable solutions for complicated issues. She has devoted her life work to helping people break free from their procrastinating behavior in order to launch their greatest work.

Karyn transfers her knowledge of the power of decisive action through keynote addresses, workshops and speeches. These presentations gives you the boost of confidence, courage, clarity and action steps needed to bring out the skills you already have and get you moving forward and upward.

In addition to her dynamic and engaging presentations, Karyn provides

- One on one coaching
- Implementation and execution training for sales departments and department managers
- Individual and group productivity training
- Customized business leader development programs

Karyn is eager to help you fully integrate the Business Wait Loss concepts into your business. She can be reached through her website, email at KB@KarynBuggs.com, or by calling (330) 249-1880.

www.ingramcontent.com/pod-product-compliance
Lightning Source LLC
Chambersburg PA
CBHW060614210326
41520CB00010B/1332